TEACHER'S RESOUR

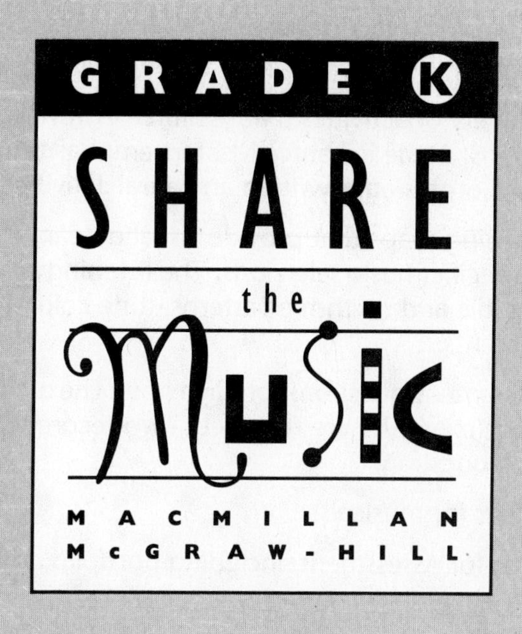

SERIES AUTHORS

Judy Bond
Coordinating Author

René Boyer-White

Margaret Campbelle-duGard

Marilyn Copeland Davidson
Coordinating Author

Robert de Frece

Mary Goetze
Coordinating Author

Doug Goodkin

Betsy M. Henderson

Michael Jothen

Carol King

Vincent P. Lawrence
Coordinating Author

Nancy L. T. Miller

Ivy Rawlins

Susan Snyder
Coordinating Author

Macmillan/McGraw-Hill School Publishing Company
New York • Columbus

INTRODUCTION

This ***Teacher's Resource Masters*** book contains supplementary activities for ***Share the Music.***

The Resource Masters include the following:

- A variety of activities that reinforce or review concepts taught in the lessons. Some Resource Masters emphasize manipulative activities, while others offer written and aural activities.
- Listening maps that provide visual guidance for students as they listen to specific music selections. The listening maps help students identify melodic and rhythmic patterns, tone color, form, and other musical elements.
- Assessment questions for each unit. The assessment questions and music examples are recorded. Two recorded options are available for each question.
- Scripts for musicals.
- Tools for Assessment, including portfolio and self-assessment forms.
- An answer key.

All Resource Masters may be duplicated for classroom use. Each is keyed into the Teacher's Edition. A line at the bottom of the Resource Master identifies the page in the Teacher's Edition with which the Resource Master is intended to be used.

For listening maps, teaching suggestions are provided on the back of the Resource Master.

ACKNOWLEDGMENTS

Grateful acknowledgment is given to the following authors, composers, and publishers. Every effort has been made to trace the ownership of all copyrighted material and to secure the necessary permissions to reprint these selections. In the case of some selections for which acknowledgment is not given, extensive research has failed to locate the copyright holders.

Basia Jaworski for *Jack and Jill* by Basia Jaworski. Copyright © 1993 by Basia Jaworski.

Jack Cardinal Mat'o for *Winter Count* by Jack Cardinal Mat'o. Copyright © 1993 by Jack G. Cardinal Mat'o.

Macmillan/McGraw-Hill School Division
10 Union Square East
New York, New York 10003

Printed in the United States of America

ISBN 0-02-295085-0 / K

1 2 3 4 5 6 7 8 9 MAL 99 98 97 96 95 94

Table of Contents

Name ____________________

Drawing Body Parts

Children complete the drawing and name the parts of the body.

Name ______________________________

RESOURCE MASTER 1•2 Practice

Four Ways to Use the Voice

Working with a partner, one child points to a picture while his or her partner makes the appropriate sound.

Name ____________________

Bear Hunt

Children color and arrange pictures in story sequence.

Name

RESOURCE MASTER 1•3

Page 2

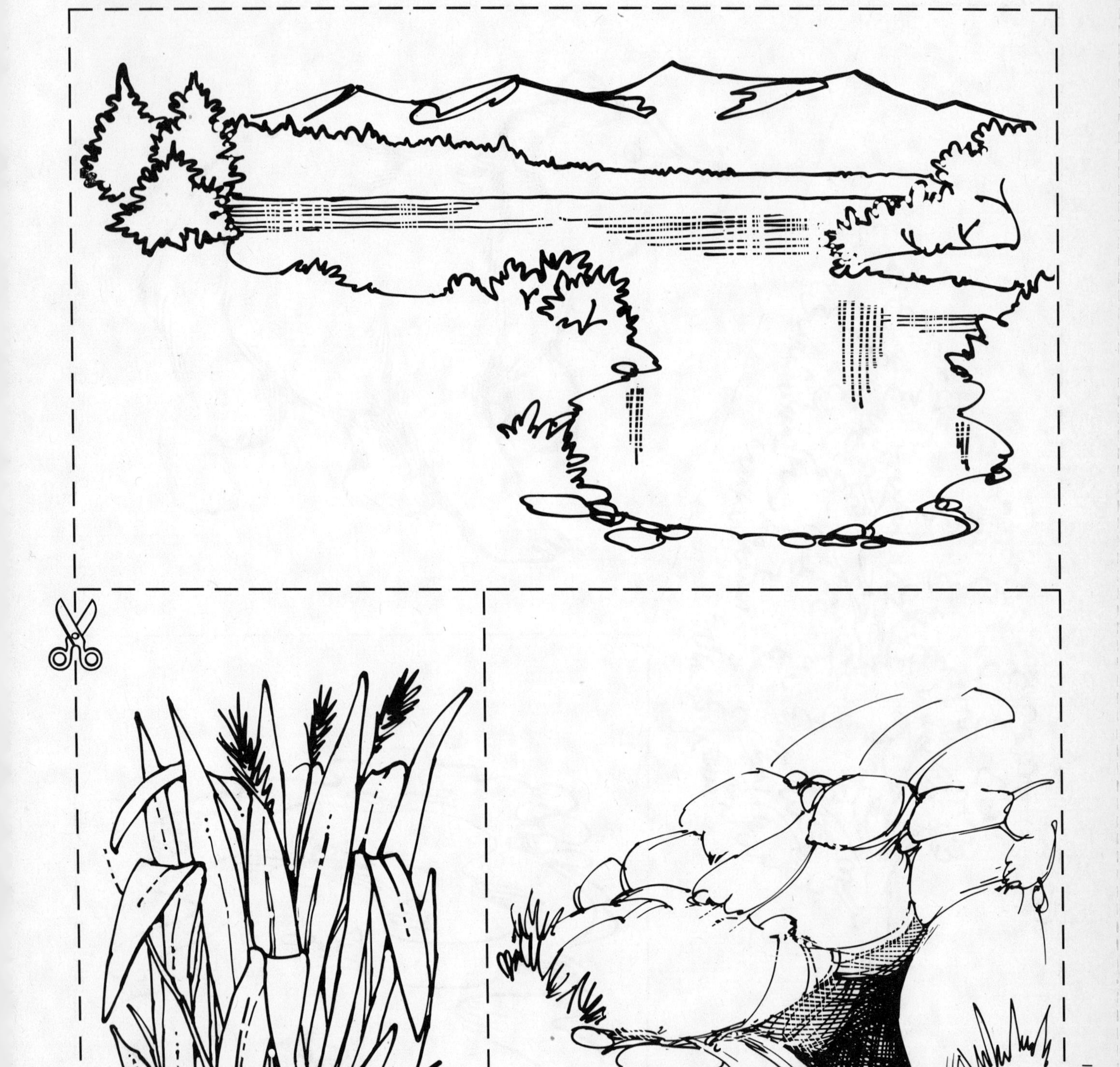

Name ____

The Roller Coaster

by Marta Sanchez

USING RESOURCE MASTER 1•4

DIRECTIONS:

Distribute a copy of the Resource Master to each child. Have children cut out the roller coaster car in the corner of the map. When you play the recording, have the children follow the roller coaster tracks up and down with the shape of the melody they hear.

Name ______________________________

Loud and Soft

loud

soft

Children draw a picture in each box of something that makes a loud sound or a soft sound.

Name ______________________________

RESOURCE MASTER 1•6 Assessment

Check It Out

1.

2.

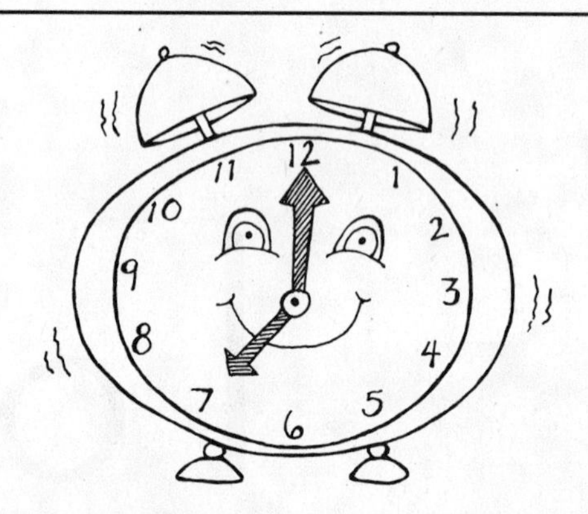

3.

4.

(See answers at the back of this book.)

Name ______________________________

Flashcards: Learning the Alphabet

A	B	C	D
E	F	G	H
I	J	K	L
M	N	O	P

Children cut out the letters and place them in random order. Sing the "Alphabet Song."

Name

RESOURCE MASTER 2•1

Page 2

Q	R	S	T
U	V	W	X
Y	Z		

Name ____

A Circle of Friends

by Sue Snyder

USING RESOURCE MASTER 2•2

DIRECTIONS:

Distribute a copy of the Resource Master to each child. Have children cut out all the squares at the bottom of the page, for use with the story. Then have children place one character's square in each blank square around the lake path as they listen to the story. The map begins with the cabin, continues counterclockwise, and ends with the meadow.

Name ____

Character Cards for "A Circle of Friends"

Children cut out cards and put them in correct sequence. Tell the story using the cards as cues.

Name ____

A Clock at Night

by Svyatoslav Miloslavskiy

USING RESOURCE MASTER 2•4

DIRECTIONS:

Distribute a copy of the Resource Master to each child. Have children find the two pictures on the listening map that are the same (clocks) and the one picture that is different (the boy looking out the window). Have them color the clocks one color and the boy in the window another color to highlight same and different sections.

Name ____________________

Check It Out

1.

A

B

2.

A

B

3.

4.

(See answers at the back of this book.)

Name ____________________

RESOURCE MASTER 2•6 Script

Winter Beads

A young boy goes to the lodge of his grandmother and scratches upon the door. She lets him in. It was during the time of the popping tree and the boy's feet were cold from the winter snow. As the boy entered the lodge, he circled to the left, to the right, and then he sat at the right arm of his grandmother. She was sitting by the fire, beading.

The boy looked down and said "Grandmother, is it true that the beads you put on my father's war shirt tell us a story of his bravery and all the great things he has done?"

"Yes, grandson, it is true. All the beads tell a story. Each one tells it's own story. Each bead tells you something if you can read it. In the season of short days and long nights, there is snow on the ground. So, I use the white beads for the background of the story I wish to tell. All that see it will know that the white beads used in the work mean that it was done in winter time.

"Yellow is a beautiful color. Most beading with this color represents the Sun or Eagle. That is why we put the tepees facing East so when the sun comes up and wakes us, we can greet the four directions one by one, warm our bodies with the kiss of the morning sun and send our prayers on the wings of Wambli (spotted Eagle) to the Great Spirit (Waken Tanka).

Have children take the story home. They can enjoy listening to a family member read it aloud.

"And blue, blue beads tell us that there is a blue sky or blue water. Or, it can also tell us that blue is the color of the tear that is shed by a mother for a young one in happiness or in sorrow. The blue is a sky that shines above us, where the Wambli (spotted Eagle) writes his name on the wind.

"Red is the color many Indian women use to color the scalp where they part their hair to show that they walk the path of Mother Earth and give new life.

"Now, we have other colors, too. From the circle unbroken, we have the mouse. It is green, for when the mouse runs through the tall buffalo grass all he can see is green. When we are born we are mice, we can only see the tall grass before our faces. As we move in our circle to the movement of the sun, we become the wolf cub. Our Grandfathers tell us many things, our Uncles teach us many things, our Grandmothers show us many things. Each movement in the circle is a new adventure in our lives.

"So you see, each bead tells its own story, and you have gained something from each bead as it is sewn. It is like a seed of life, the circle unbroken. Everything that has been given to us has been given to us by the Great Spirit, even the colors of the rainbow."

Name ________________________________

RESOURCE MASTER 2•7 Practice

Bead Patterns

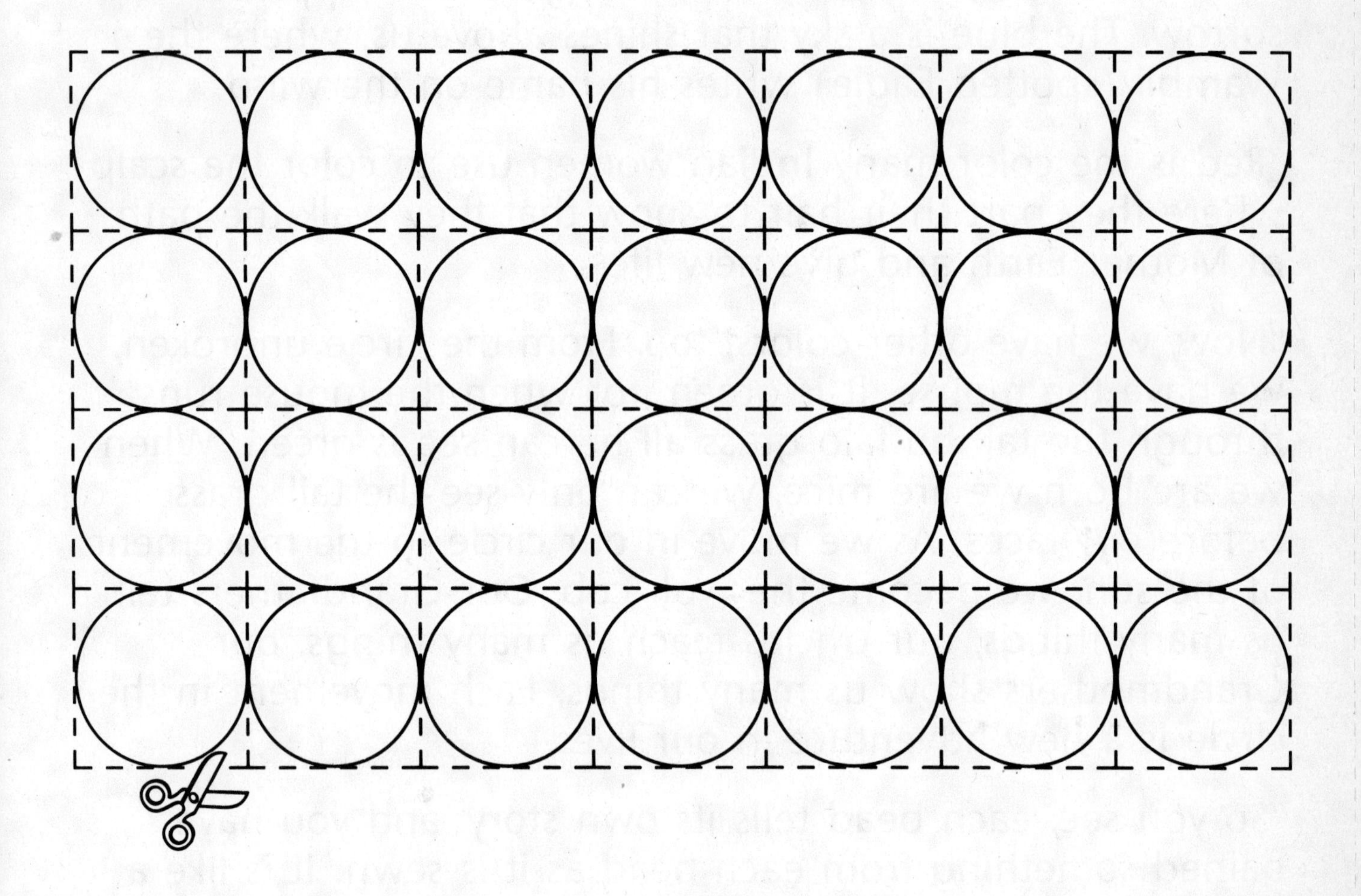

Children use different colors to fill the circles. Cut and arrange the squares in different patterns. Have the children glue their favorite pattern on paper.

Name ___________________________

Long and Short

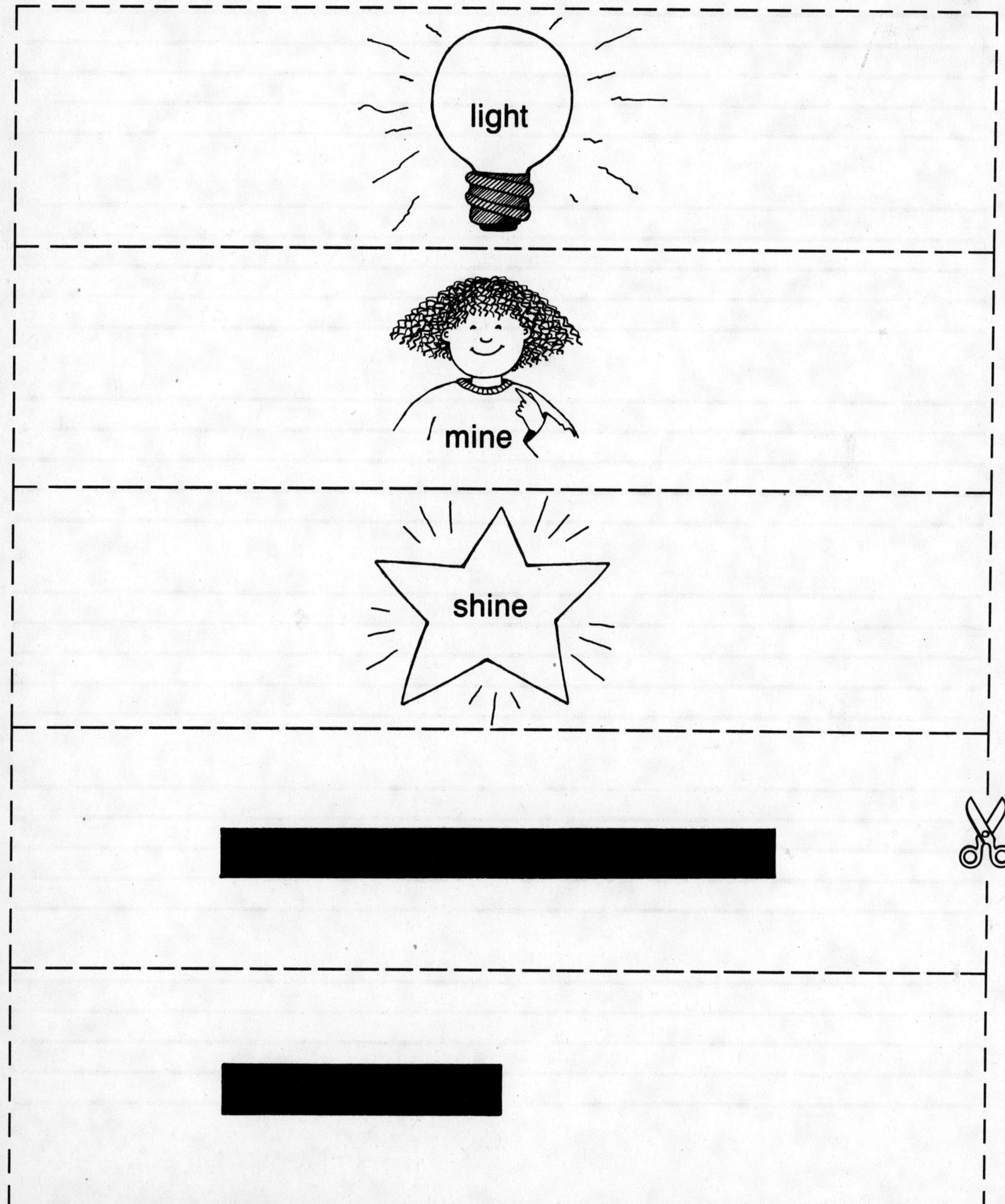

Children choose a card. Say the word with them. Point to the icon which describes the word as long or short.

Name ______________________________

Ballet of the Unhatched Chicks
from *Pictures at an Exhibition*

by Modest Mussorgsky

USING RESOURCE MASTER 3•2

DIRECTIONS:

Distribute a copy of the Resource Master to each child. Have children find the mother hens and the baby chicks in their shells on the listening map. Each chick represents one phrase of music on the recording. The chick section is characterized by very active music with many short notes played by woodwinds. Point out and say *peep!* for all three locations of this word on the map. This represents a sudden high note played by the woodwinds at the end of a phrase. The less frantic march of the large hen represents the less frantic music of the middle section, played by strings. Then the frantic little chick melody returns, ending in a few short high woodwind notes represented by the final "peep!" on the listening map.

Name ____

Slavonic Dance Op. 46, No. 1 (excerpt)

by Antonín Dvořák

USING RESOURCE MASTER 3•3

DIRECTIONS:

Distribute a copy of the Resource Master to each child. Have children tell the difference between the first and last couple, and the middle couple. (the first and last couples walk calmly; the middle couple jog) Ask children what they think they will hear from looking at the listening map, in terms of fast and slow in this selection. You may wish to have children color the first and last couples one color, and the middle couple a different color, to highlight same and different sections.

Name ______________________________

Poems

______________ the ______________ is a ______________.

______________ the ______________ is a ______________.

______________ the ______________ is a ______________.

And __________ the ______________ is ______________.

Using "Sleeping Outdoors" as a model, children create place poems. Fill in the blanks with place and object words. Have children create movement and instrument parts that they dictate.

Name ______________________________

RESOURCE MASTER 3•5 Assessment

Check It Out

1.

high

low

2.

high

low

3.

4.

5.

(See answers at the back of this book.)

Name ____________________

The Bus

Children arrange pictures to represent each verse.

Name ____________________

RESOURCE MASTER 4•1

Page 2

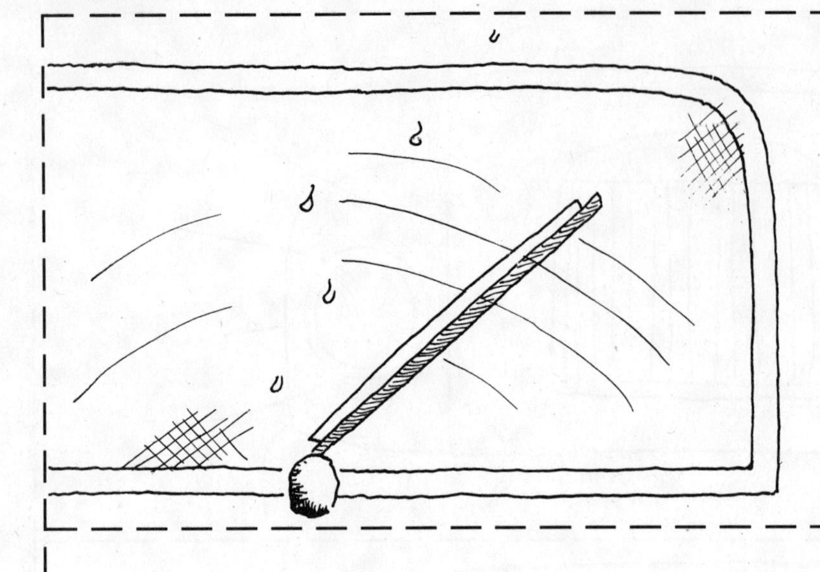

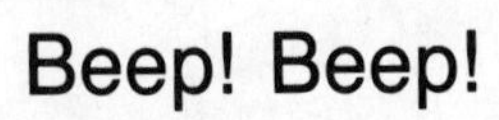

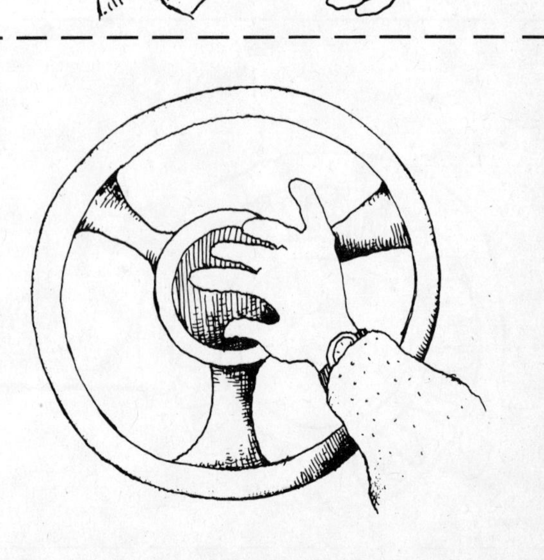

Name ________________________________

Engine, Engine Number Nine

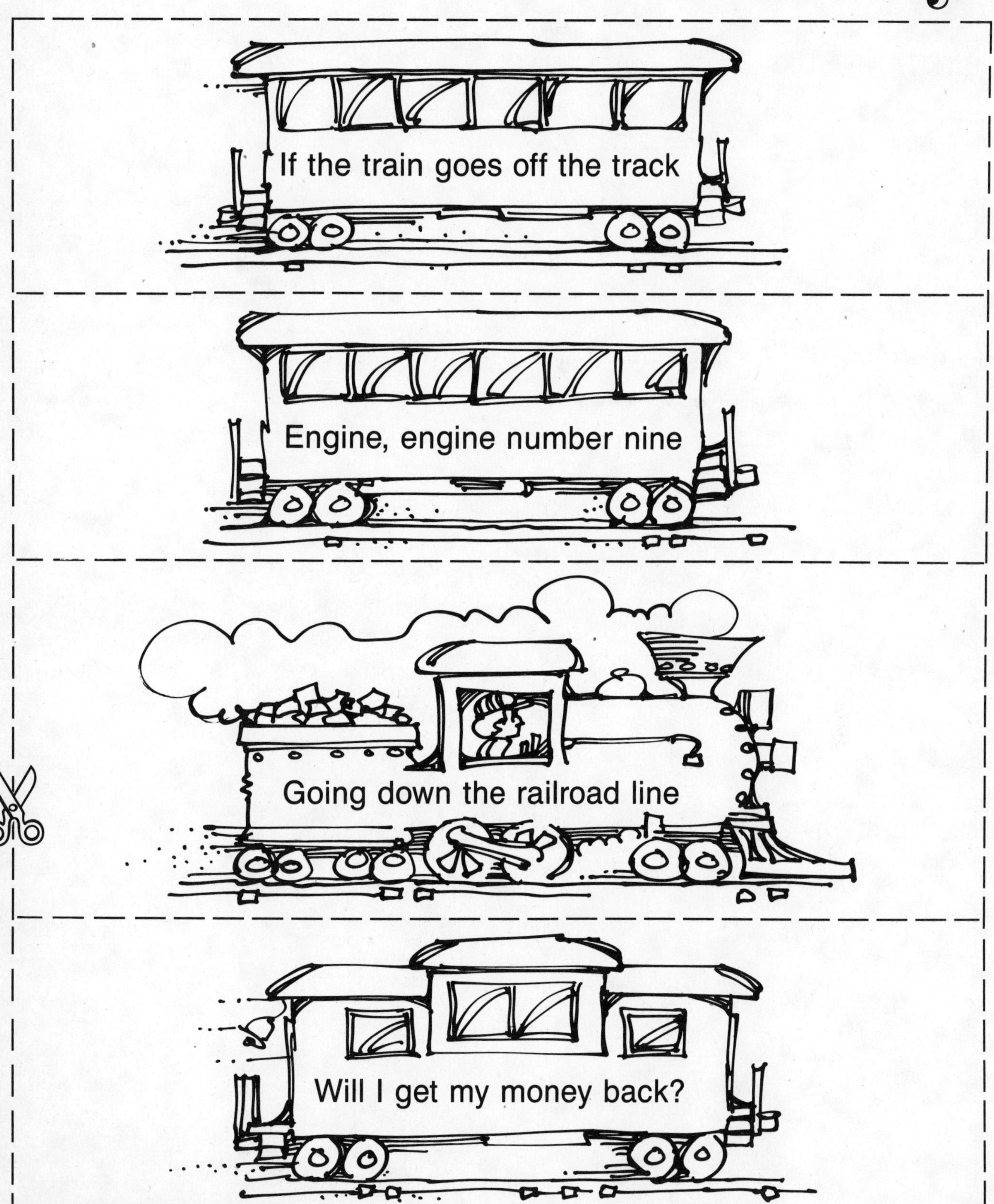
If the train goes off the track
Engine, engine number nine
Going down the railroad line
Will I get my money back?

Children arrange the train cars in verse order.

Name

RESOURCE MASTER 4•3 Practice

Car Song

Children connect the dots, and then trace the melodic direction as they sing "Car Song."

Name ____________________

Melodic Shapes for Vocal Exploration

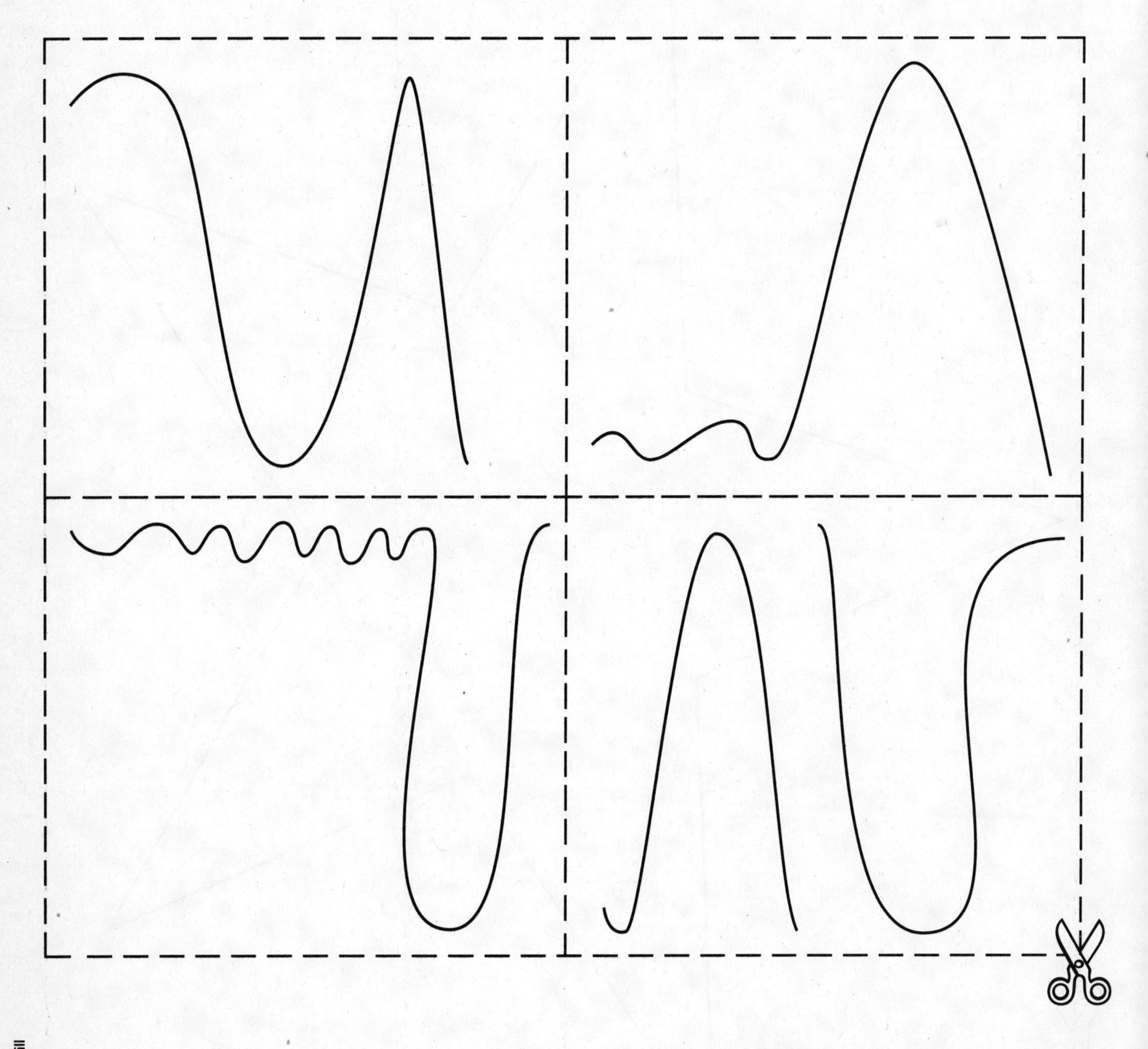

Divide class into four groups. Give each group a different pattern. Children perform sound for their pattern. Rotate groups so that children can perform all patterns.

Name ______

RESOURCE MASTER 4•5 Practice

Melodic Shape

Choose fourteen children to hold the stars. Have them arrange the stars by holding them at different levels to show the melodic contour of the first phrase of "Twinkle, Twinkle, Little Star." Repeat activity so each child has a turn.

Name ____________________

Check It Out

1.

2.

3.

4.

5.

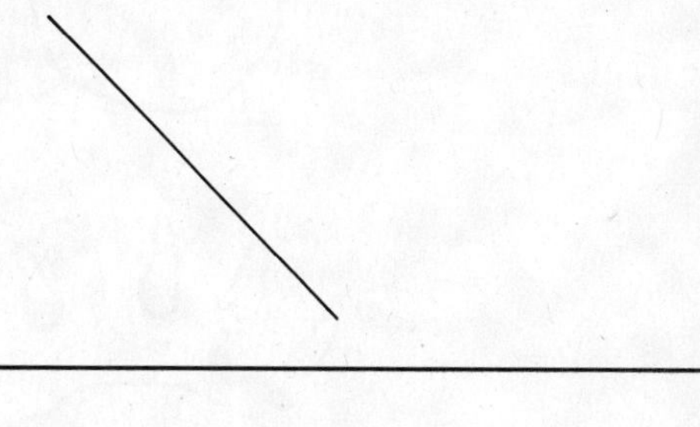

6.

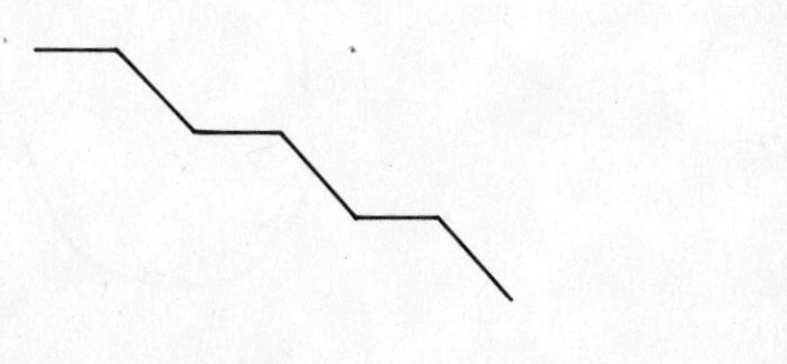

(See answers at the back of this book.)

Name ____________________

RESOURCE MASTER 5•1 Practice

Animal Tracks

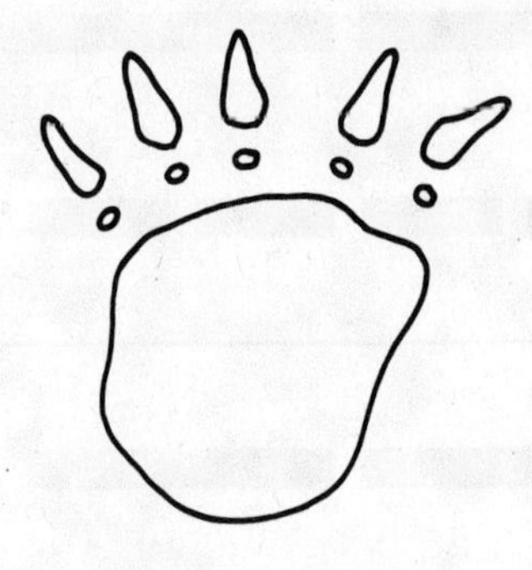

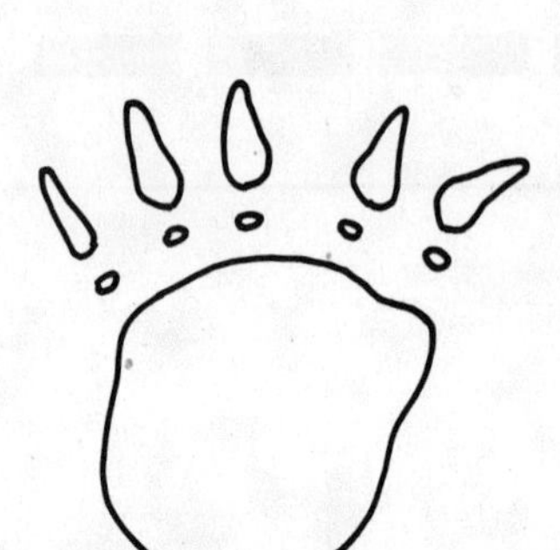

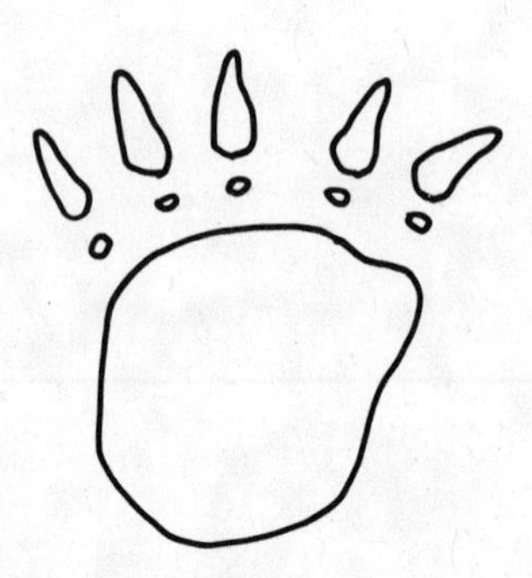

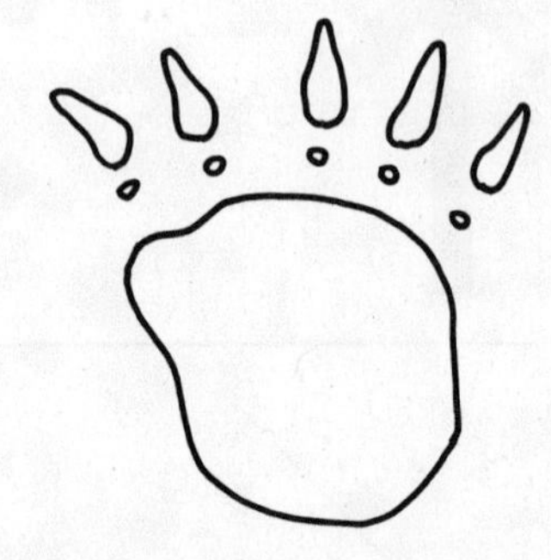

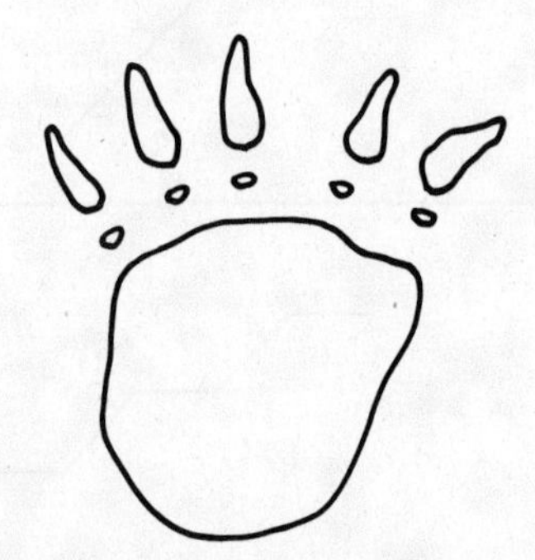

Children color the brontosaurus tracks. Have them point to the tracks with the beat as they sing the last two phrases of "Oh, A-Hunting We Will Go."

Name ____________________

Little Ducky Duddle

As children sing "Little Ducky Duddle," they point to one duck on each beat.

Name ____________________

RESOURCE MASTER 5•3 Practice

Three Little Fishies: Stick Puppets

Children color the figures. Paste them to craft sticks to make the puppets. Use puppets to dramatize the song.

Name ____

Check It Out

1.

2.

3.

4.

(See answers at the back of this book.)

Name ______________________________

RESOURCE MASTER 6•1 Practice

"El florón" Game

Children use the flower while playing the game.

Name ______________________________

Creating Four-Beat Rhythms (I)

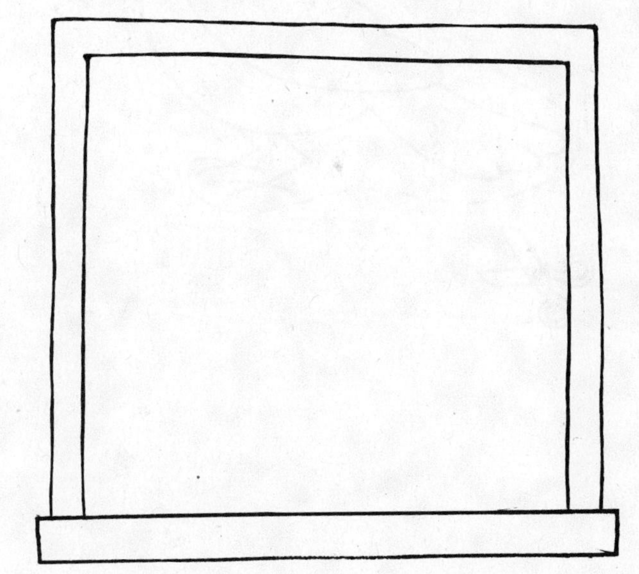

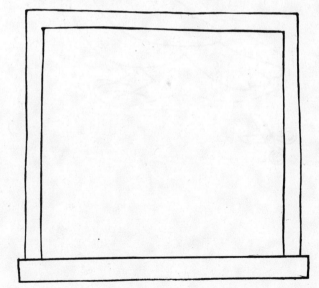

Children place birds from page 42 in windows to create four-beat rhythm combinations.

Name ________________________________

RESOURCE MASTER 6•2

Page 2

Name ______________________________

Creating Four-Beat Rhythms (II)

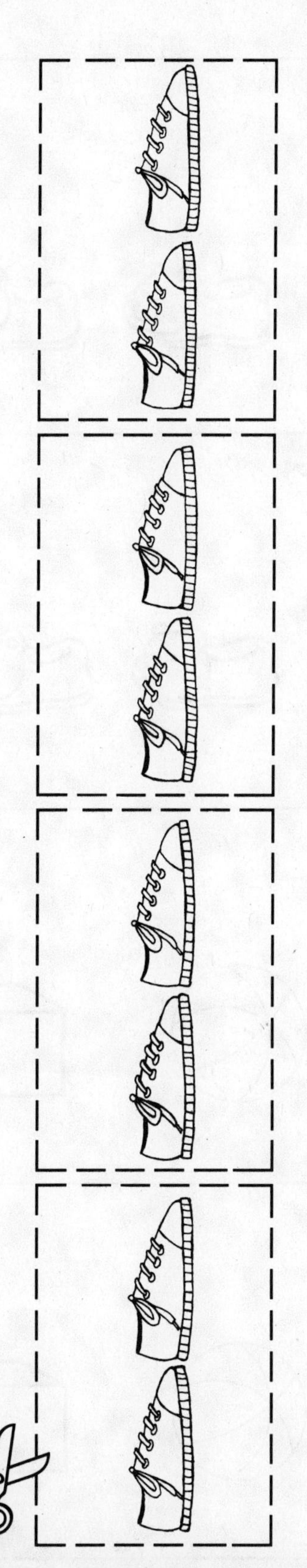

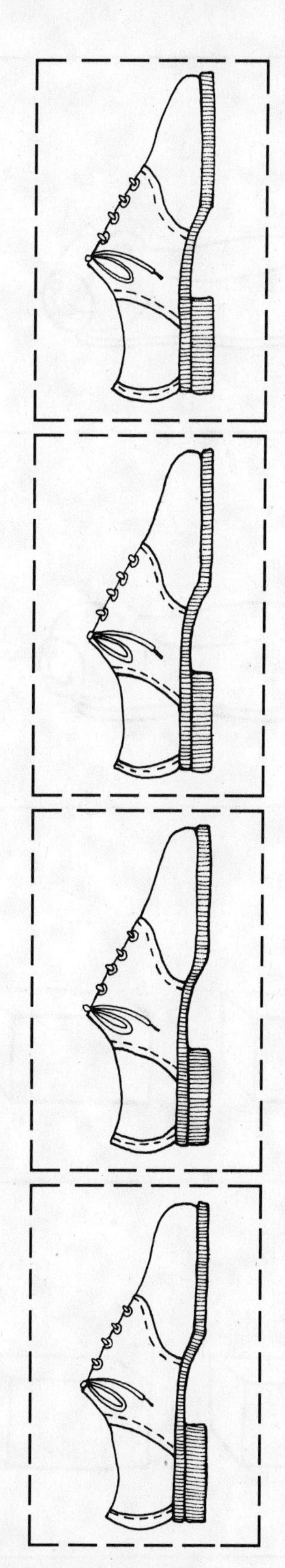

Children use the pictures to create different four-beat combinations.

Name ____________________

RESOURCE MASTER 6•4 Assessment

Check It Out

1. 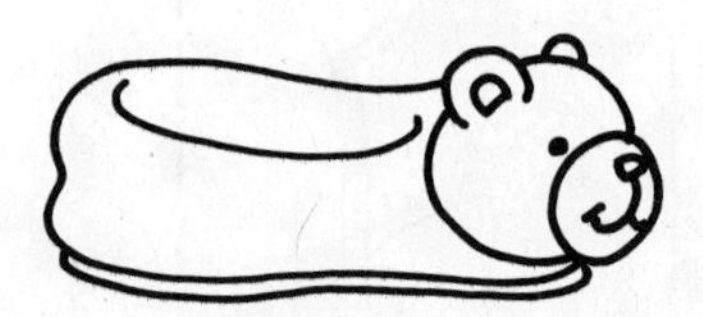	
2. 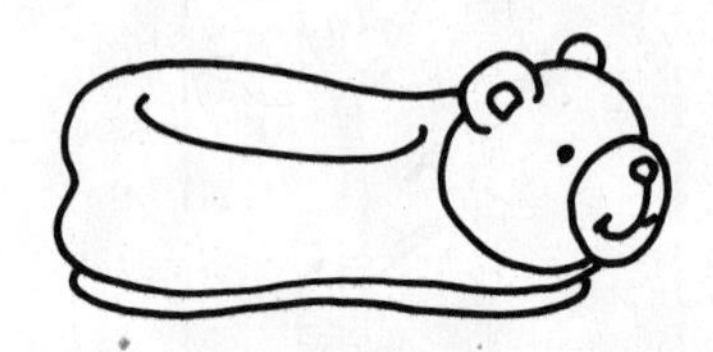	
3. 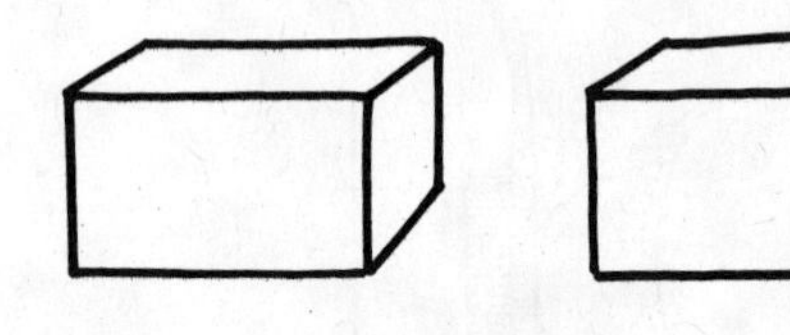	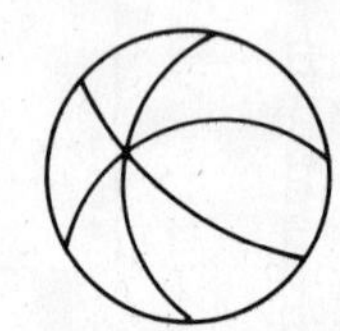 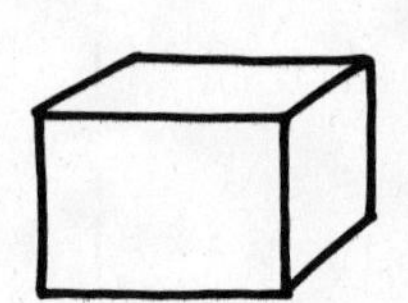
4. 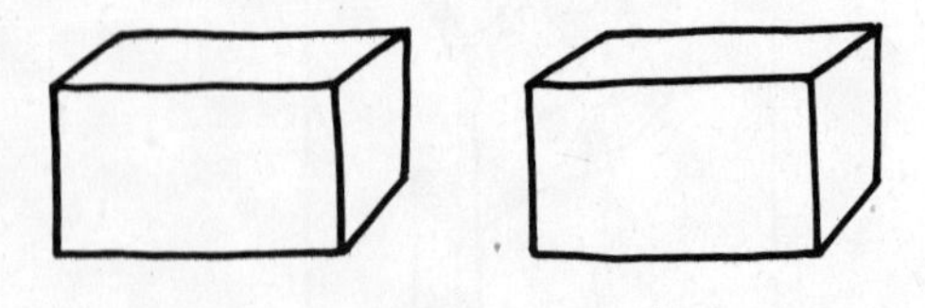	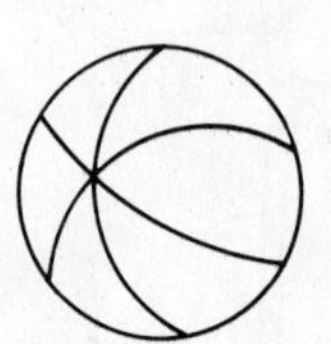 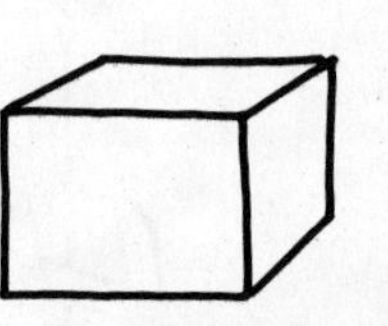

(See answers at the back of this book.)

Name ____________________

Make a Flag

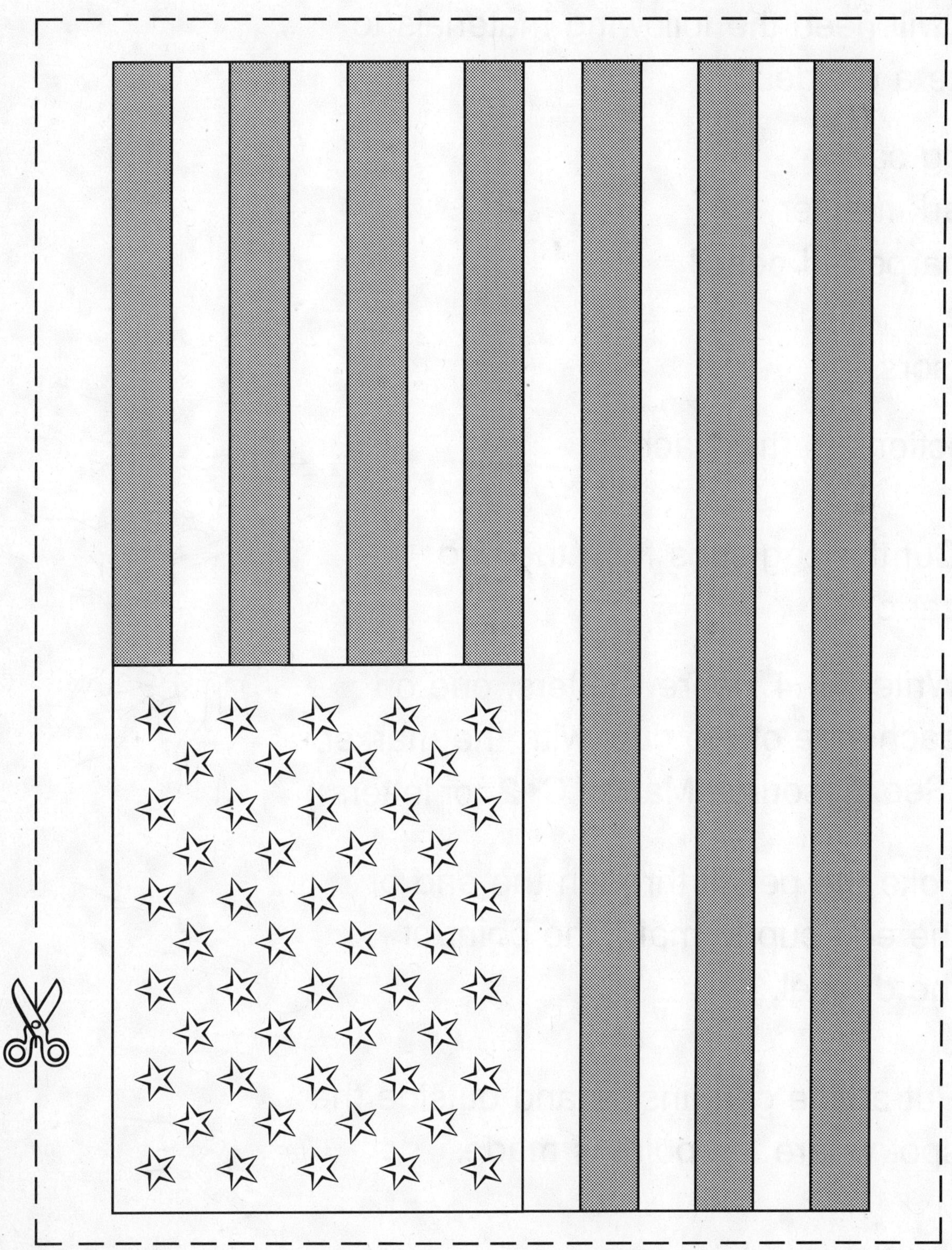

Children make flags to use in their parades.

Name ______________________________

RESOURCE MASTER C•2 Practice

Make a Dreidel

You will need the following materials to make a dreidel:

1 egg carton
1 dark marker
1 sharpened pencil
glue
scissors

Directions to the teacher:

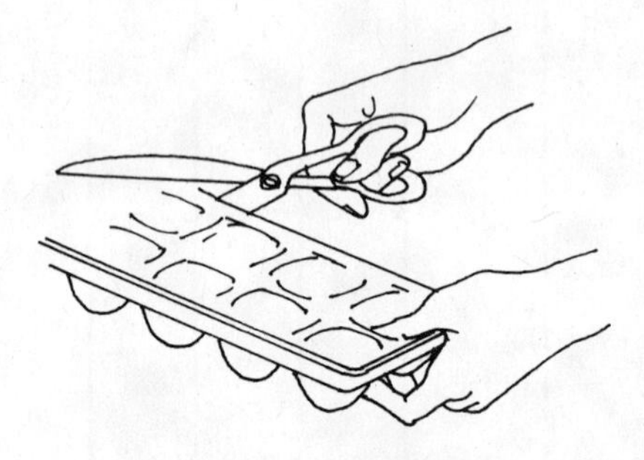

1. Cut the egg cups from the egg carton.

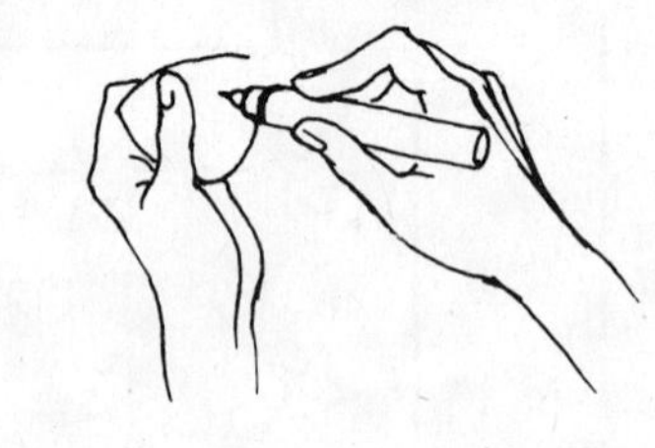

2. Write the 4 Hebrew letters, one on each side of the cup, with the marker. (See Resource Master C•2 for letters.)

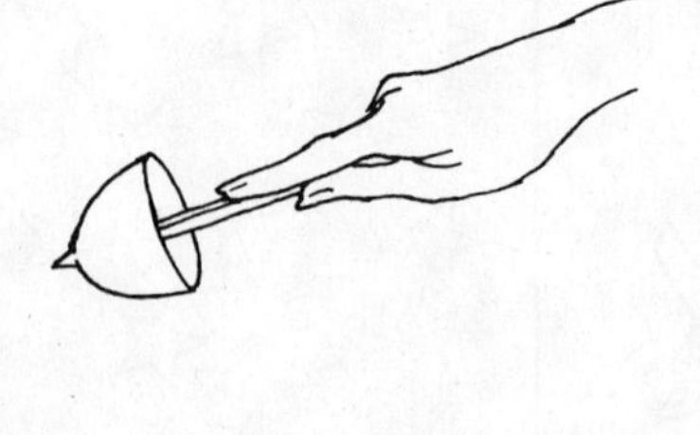

3. Poke the pencil through the end of the egg cup to make the point of the dreidel.

4. Put a little glue inside and outside the spot where the point is made.

5. Let the dreidel dry.

Name ____________________

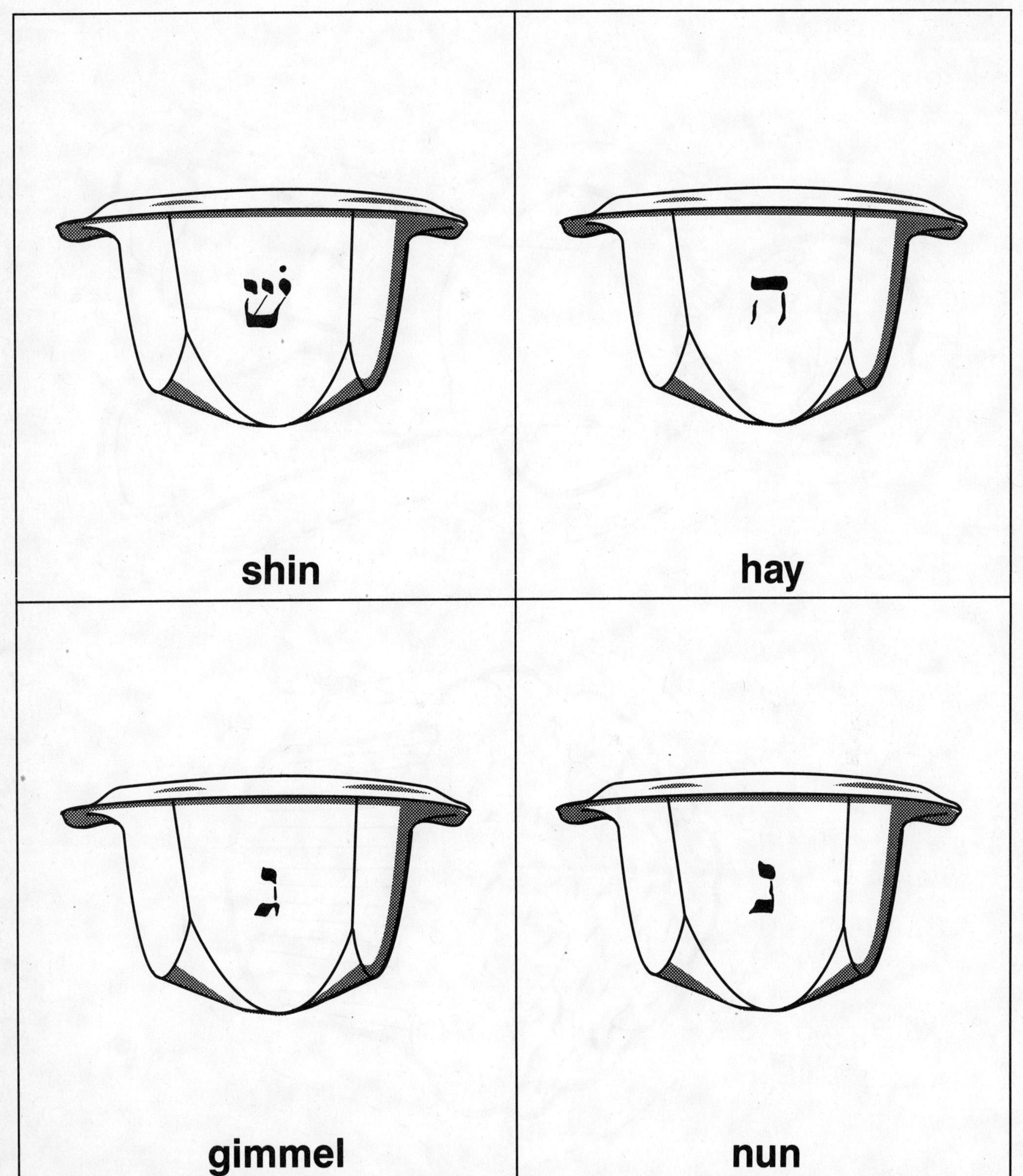

The dreidel has a Hebrew letter on each side. When the top falls, the letter turned upward tells how much the player has won or lost of the "money" called *Hanukkah gelt.* The letters are: *nun,* take none; *hay,* take half; *shin,* put one in; *gimmel,* take all. Use these letters on the sides of the dreidels.

Name ______________________________

RESOURCE MASTER SA•1 Patterns

Three Little Muffins

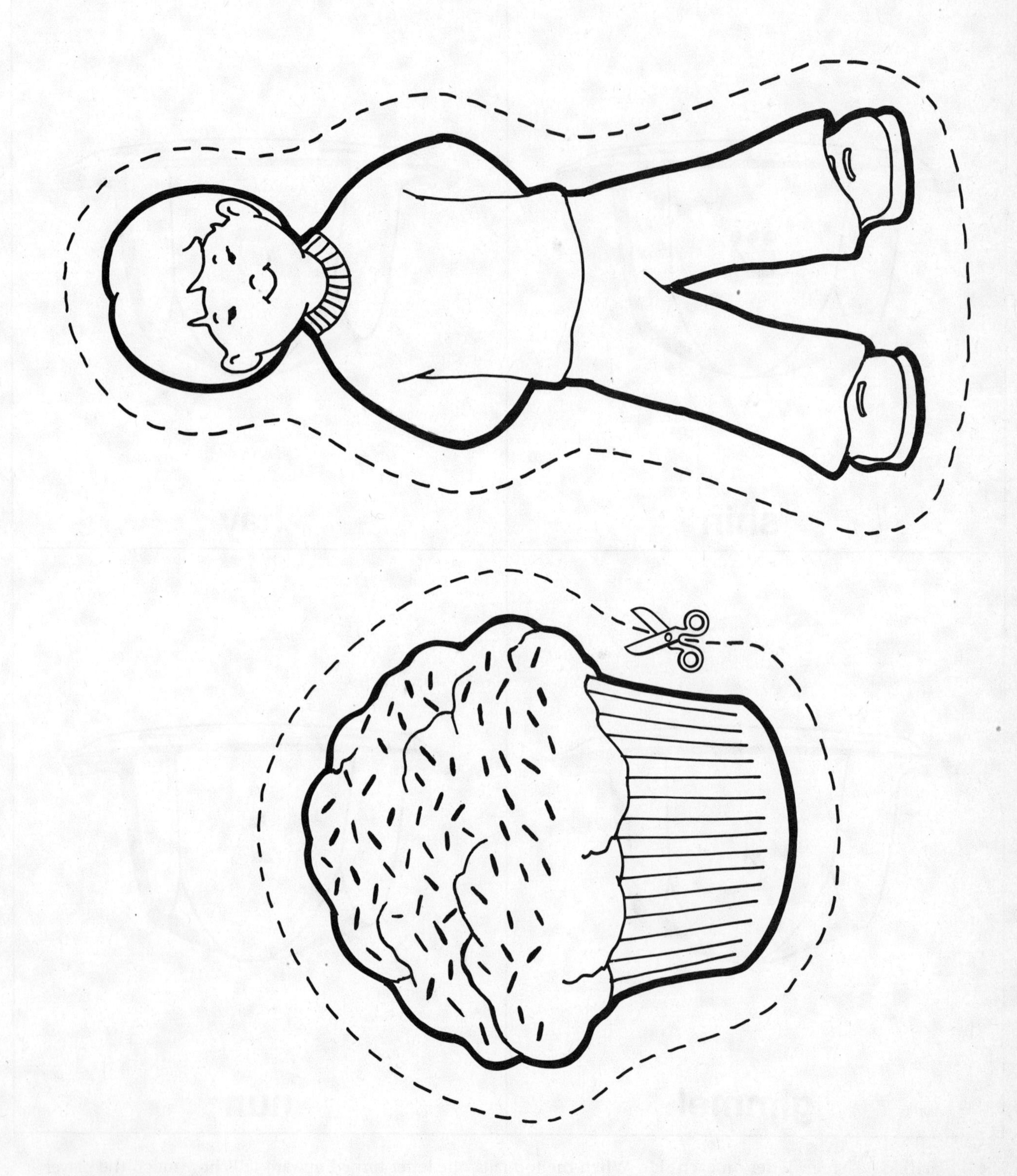

Children color and glue pictures to craft sticks. (Children will need three muffins.) Use the puppets in presenting "Three Little Muffins."

Name ______________________________

Page 2

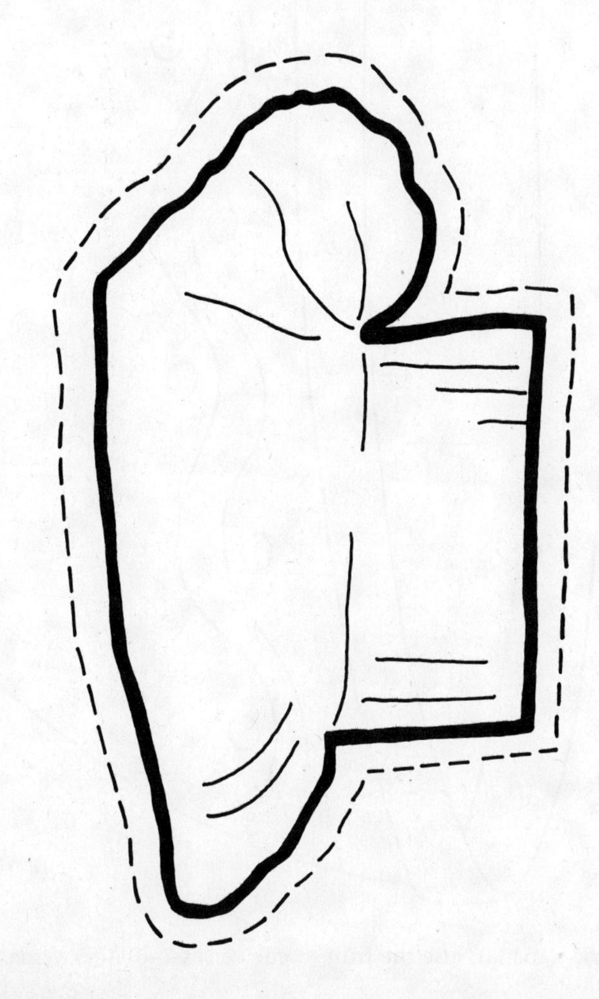

Name ____________________

RESOURCE MASTER SA•2 Practice

Apples and Bananas

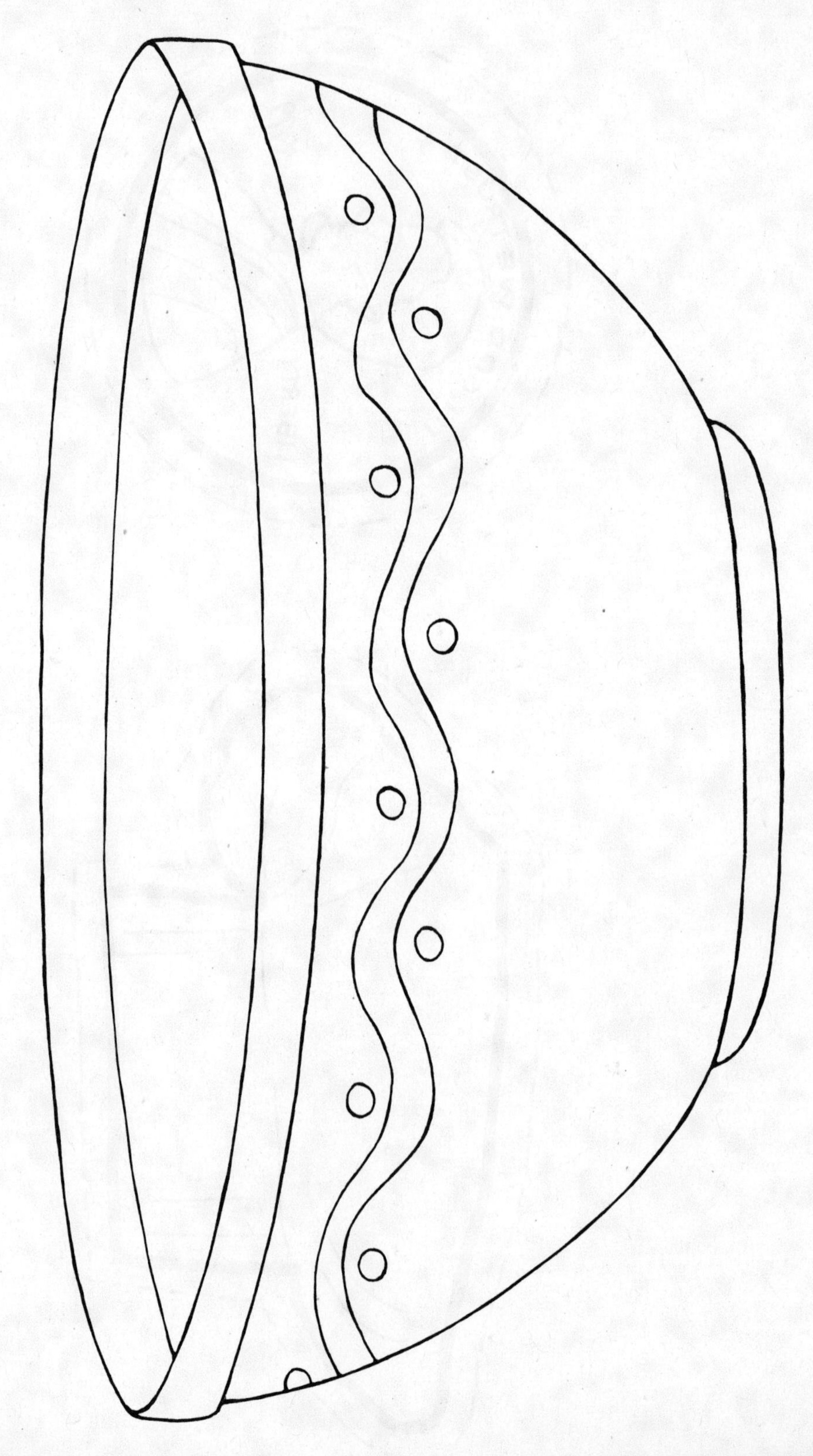

As children sing "Apples and Bananas," use the fruit to cue verses 2–6. Afterwards, children can color fruit and arrange it in the bowl.

Name ____________________

Page 2

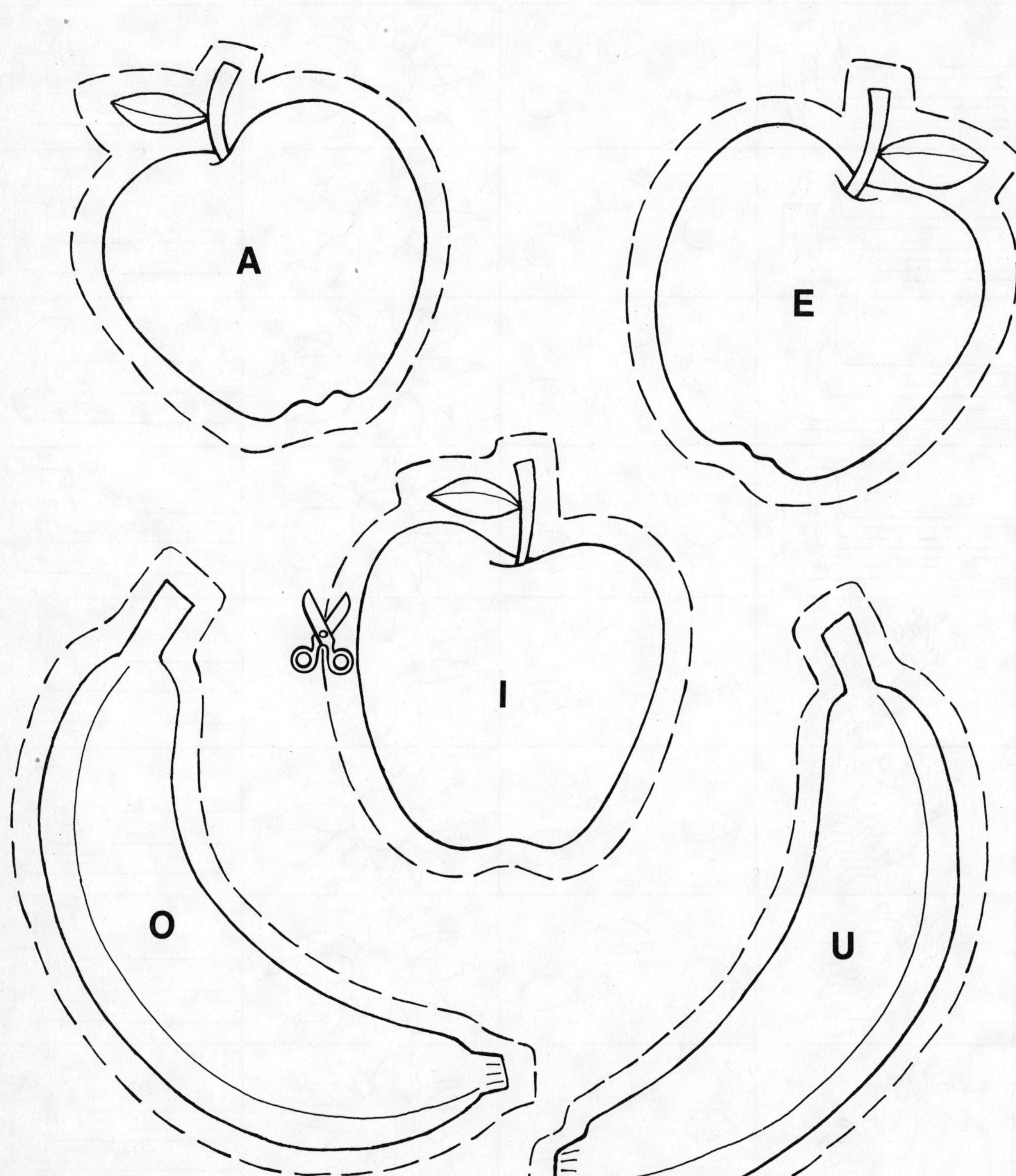

Name ____________________

RESOURCE MASTER SA•3 Practice

Pointing the Beat with the Spider

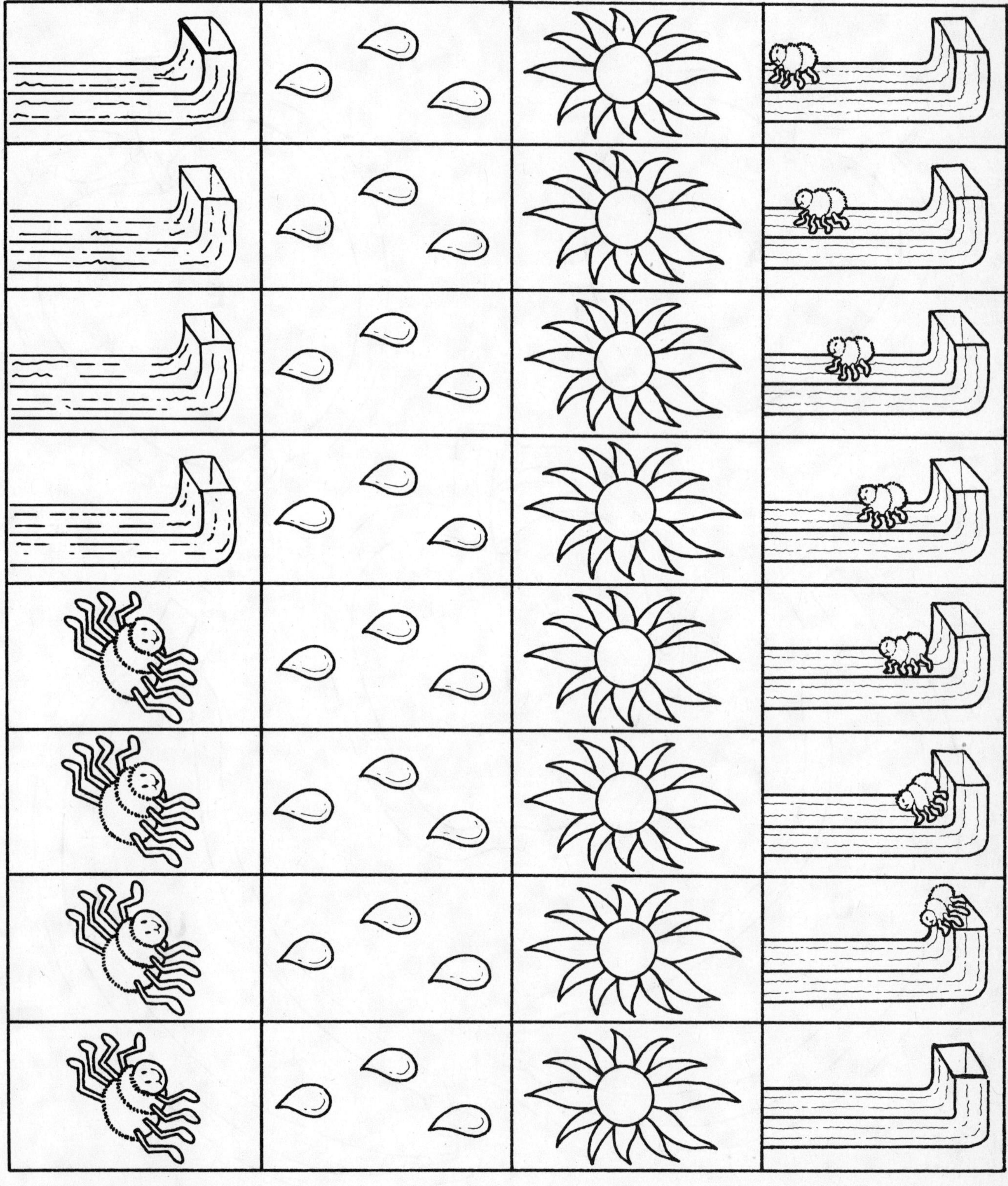

Start here

Children point to each picture as they sing "Eency Weency Spider."

Name ____

If You're Happy

If you're happy and you know it

clap your hands ____________________________

tap your foot ____________________________

nod your head ____________________________

then your face will surely show it

Children cut out pictures from page 54 and put them in verse order. Match the picture with the action in the verse.

Name ____

RESOURCE MASTER SA•4

Page 2

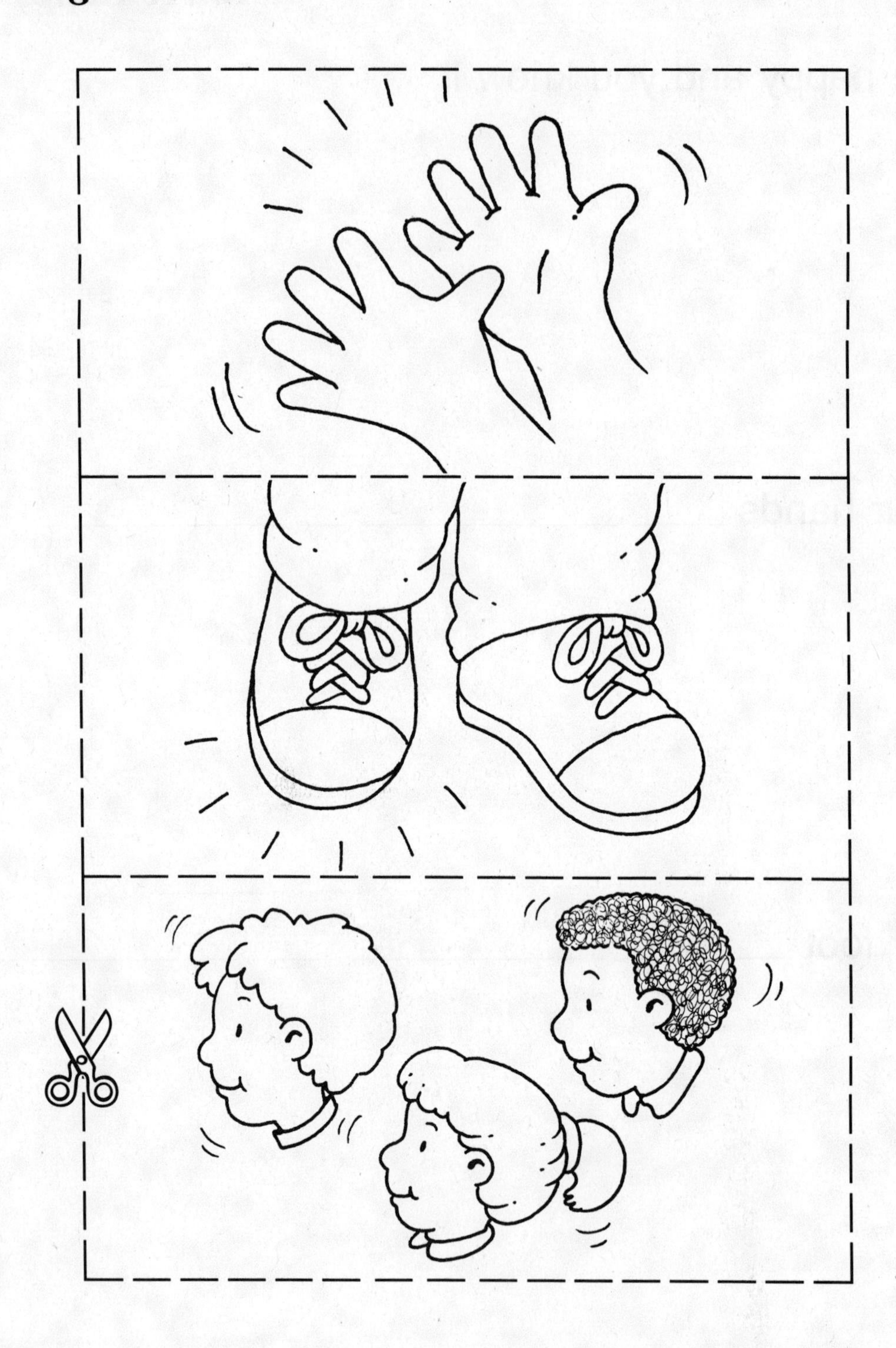

Macmillan/McGraw-Hill

Name ____________________

Fun in the Kitchen

Choose a special time to prepare and enjoy this recipe with your family and friends.

2 cups sifted whole wheat flour
3 teaspoons low-sodium baking powder
½ teaspoon salt

⅓ cup corn oil
⅔ cup milk

Sift dry ingredients together.
Add the oil.
Add the milk.

Stir until dough leaves sides of bowl. Knead lightly 15 times. Roll out ½ inch thick on floured board. Cut with biscuit cutter. Place the biscuits on an oiled cookie sheet. Bake 12 to 15 minutes at 400°.

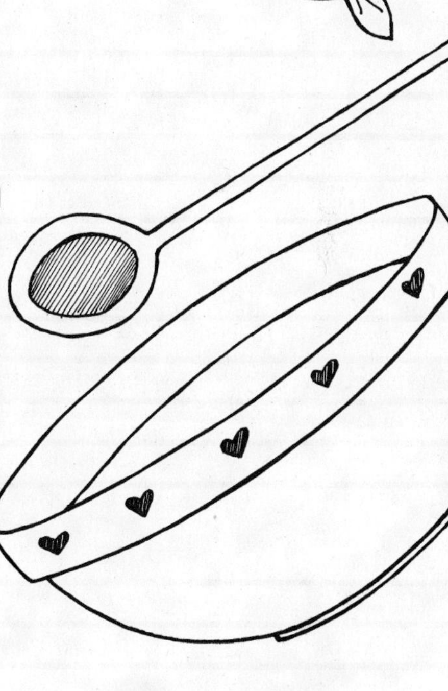

Yield: 12 biscuits.

Name ______________________________

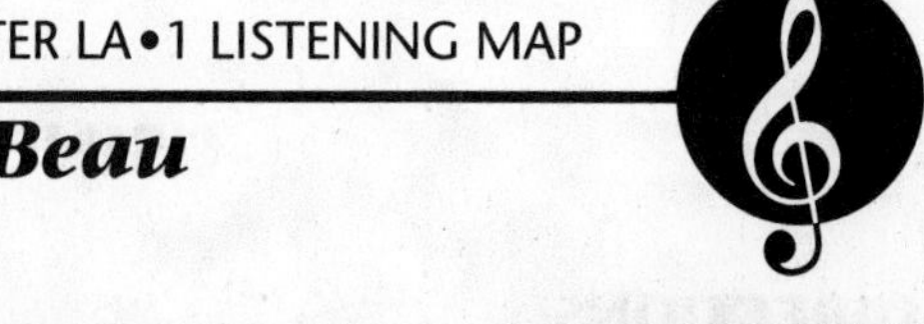

Air from *The Married Beau*

by Henry Purcell

USING RESOURCE MASTER LA•1

DIRECTIONS:

Distribute a copy of the Resource Master to each child. Ask children what all of the pictures have in common. (each shows air or wind blowing something) Tell them the title of this selection (Air), and that hundreds of years ago *air* meant *song*, and gradually came to mean a tune sung or played on instruments. Ask children if air is needed to sing. Explain that air passes through the vocal chords to produce sound. There are four main sections in this selection, one for each picture. You may also wish to have children draw other pictures of air or wind related subjects while listening to this selection.

Name ______________________________

March for the Royal Philharmonic Society (excerpt)

by Franz Joseph Haydn

Get set.
8 beats

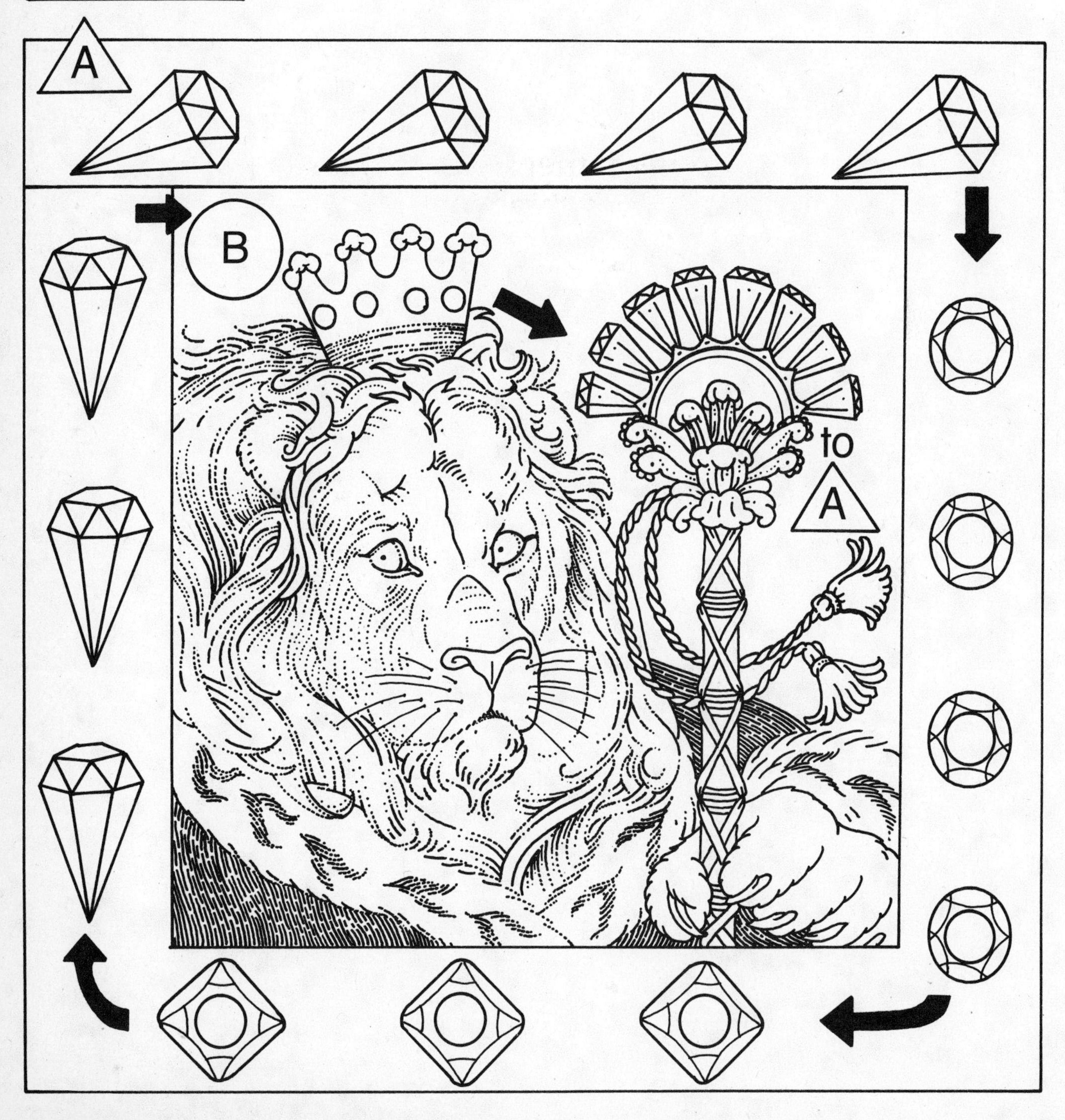

USING RESOURCE MASTER LA•2

DIRECTIONS:

Distribute a copy of the Resource Master to each child. Each jewel on the listening map represents four beats of music. The map first follows the frame around the lion, then goes to the eight jewels in the crown, to the eight jewels of the scepter, the repeats the whole thing.

Contrasting jewel styles represent a change in mood in the music. You may wish to have children color the frame one color, and the lion and scepter another color, with each group of jewels a contrasting color, to highlight same and different sections.

Name ____

Pizzicato Polka

by Johann Strauss, Jr.

USING RESOURCE MASTER LA•3

DIRECTIONS:

Distribute a copy of the Resource Master to each child. Have children find same and different dancing couples on the listening map. (first and third couples in top row and first and third couples in bottom row are the same; second couple in each row are the same; fourth, fifth, and last couples are all different) Have children color these couples to show same and different before listening to the recording. Ask children if they think the music for the last couple will sound fast or slow. (fast) Point out and explain the signs before listening.

Name ______________________________

South Rampart Street Parade

by Steve Allen, Ray Bauduc, and Robert Haggart

USING RESOURCE MASTER LA•4

DIRECTIONS:

Distribute a copy of the Resource Master to each child. Help children to identify all the instruments on the listening map. (trumpet, trombone, drum, clarinet) The number of beats in each section is given at the bottom of each box to assist in keeping track of the beginning and end of each section.

Name ______________________________

Getting to Know You from *The King and I*

by Richard Rodgers and Oscar Hammerstein II

Macmillan/McGraw-Hill Listening Map concept by Diane Bethea Steele

USING RESOURCE MASTER LA•5

DIRECTIONS:

Distribute a copy of the Resource Master to each child. Explain the boxes to the children. (a teacher talking, a teacher singing, no singing, and children and teacher singing) Tell them to point to the picture of what they hear while listening to the recording.

Name ______________________________

Miniwanka, or The Moments of Water

by R. Murray Schafer

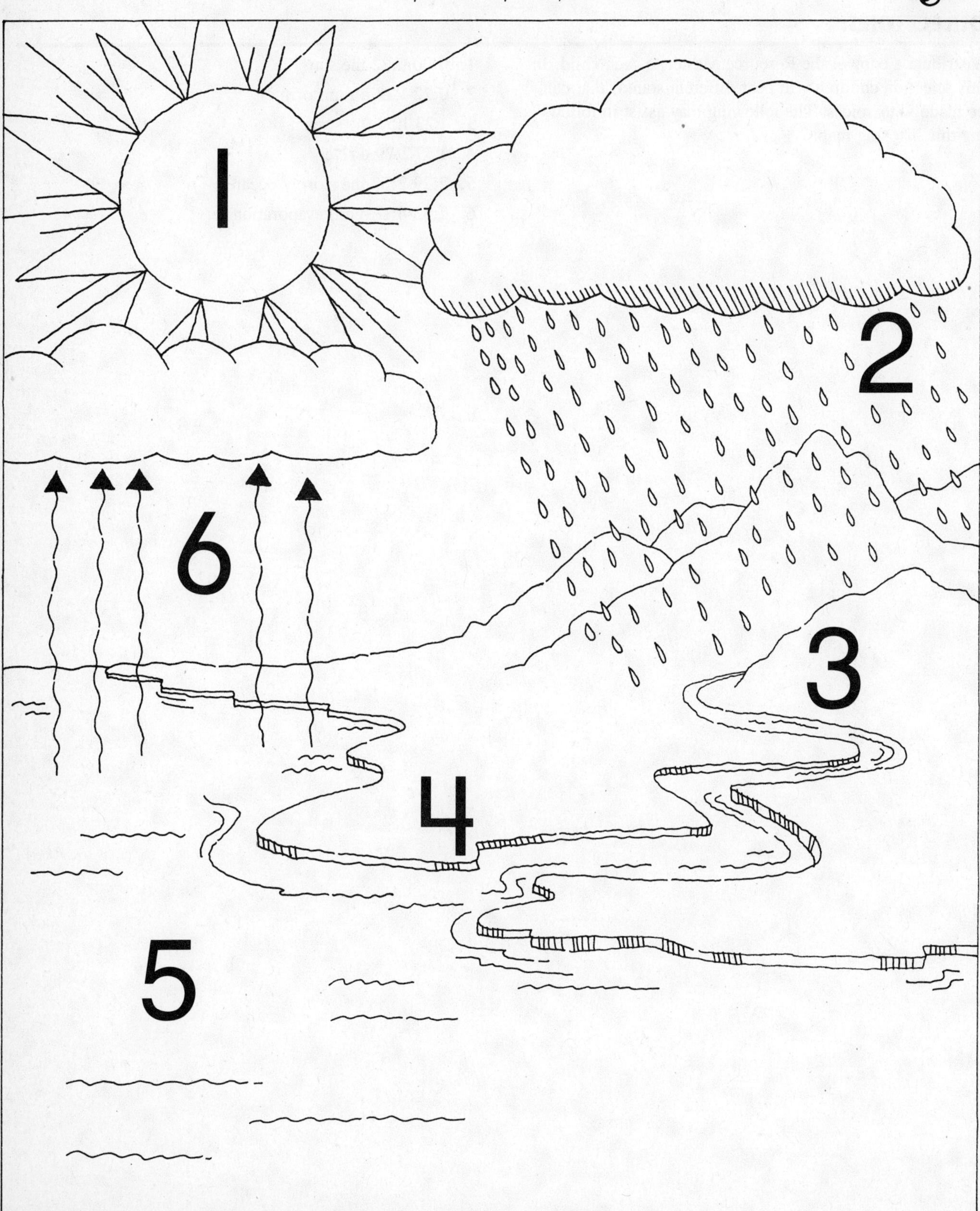

USING RESOURCE MASTER LA•6

DIRECTIONS:

Distribute a copy of the Resource Master to each child. In this selection children will hear different sounds that can be made with voices. The following may assist in following this listening map:

1. 0:00-0:22 the sun
2. 0:22-1:23 a rainstorm
3. 1:23-1:57 the stream
4. 1:57-2:29 a river
5. 2:29-2:53 the stormy ocean
6. 2:53-4:17 (end) evaporation

Name ______________________________

Jack and the Beanstalk

Traditional Folktale
Music and Text by Basia Jaworski

Cast		
Jack	Jack's Mother	Hen
Cow	Old Man	Magic Harp
Giant	Giant's Wife	

SONG: *(all)* "This Is the Story of Jack"

Narrator: Once there was a boy named Jack*, who lived with his mother* in a cottage in the country. One day, Mother* told Jack* to take the cow* to town and sell her, because they needed money for food.

SONG: *(all)* "Walking"

Name ____________________

Jack and the Beanstalk

To the teacher: As you narrate, the children can present "Jack and the Beanstalk" with masks. Prepare by distributing a copy of this mask outline to each character. Have the children decorate the masks to represent the characters, then staple the masks to flat sticks. The children "wear" the masks by holding the sticks up to their faces. Or, they can attach string to the masks and hang them around their necks. Let the children choose instruments to represent each character. They can play the instruments at the asterisks while you pause in the reading. If you wish, have the children take home a copy of the script to enjoy with grown-ups.

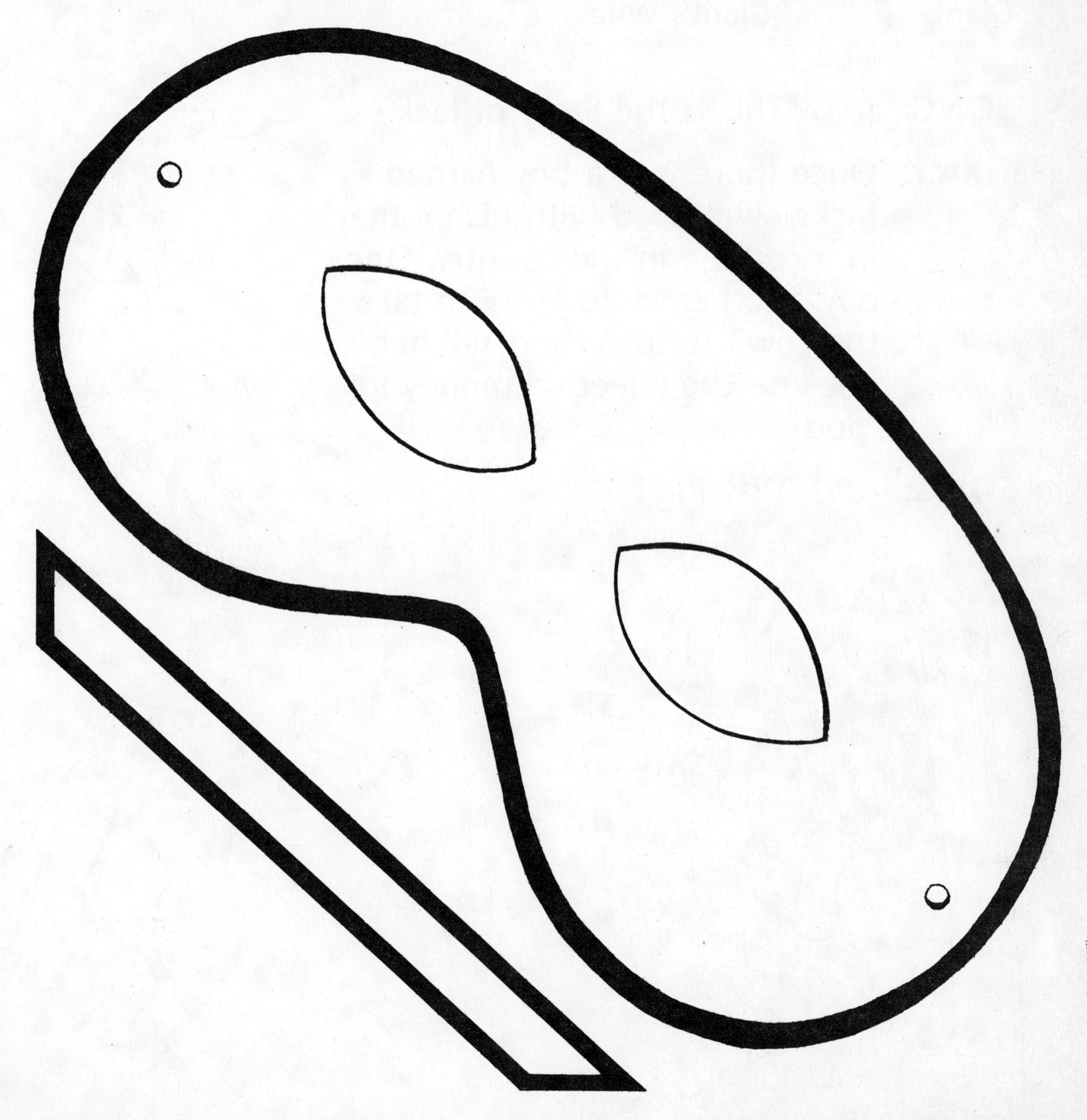

Narrator: On the way to town, Jack* met an old man.* The old man* wanted the cow* and offered to trade the cow* for some shiny beans. Jack* couldn't take his eyes off the beans, so he gave the cow* to the old man* and got the beans in return. The old man* took the cow* away, and Jack* ran home, very excited.

Jack: See what I got for the cow*, Mother*!

Narrator: When his mother* saw the beans, she was very angry. She threw the beans out the window and sent Jack* to bed without supper!

SONG: *(all)* "Poor Jack"

Narrator: The next day, Jack* looked out the window and saw a huge beanstalk that reached way up to the clouds. He decided to climb the stalk.

When he reached the top of the beanstalk, Jack* saw a large castle. He went over to the door and knocked. The giant's wife* opened the door.

Giant's Wife: Yes, my dear?

Narrator: Jack* was very hungry, so he asked for something to eat. The giant's wife* invited him in, and just as she gave him a crust of bread, they heard heavy footsteps.

Giant's Wife: Quick! Hide in the oven. My husband is coming!

SONG: *(all)* "Fee Fi Fo Fum"

Narrator: The giant's wife* said,

Giant's Wife: It's only your supper that you smell.

Narrator: So the giant* sat down and ate six roasted pigs! After supper, the giant* asked for his golden hen*. The giant* said to the hen*,

Giant: Lay!

Narrator: And the hen* laid a beautiful golden egg. The giant* said again,

Giant: Lay!

Narrator: And the hen* laid another beautiful golden egg. And once again the giant* said,

Giant: Lay!

Narrator: And once again the hen* laid another beautiful golden egg. Then the giant* fell asleep.

SONG: *(all)* "While the Giant Slept" (I)

Narrator: Jack* ran to his house and showed Mother* the golden hen*. Mother* was very happy. The next day, Jack* decided to climb the beanstalk again. At the top, he saw the large castle, went to the door, and knocked. The giant's wife* opened the door.

Giant's Wife: Yes, my dear?

Narrator: Jack* asked for something to eat, and just as the giant's wife* gave him a crust of bread, they heard heavy footsteps. Once again, Jack* hid in the oven.

SONG: *(all)* "Fee Fi Fo Fum"

Giant's Wife: It's only your supper that you smell.

Narrator: So the giant* sat down and ate his supper. When he finished, the giant* asked for his magic harp*. The harp* played and sang beautiful music until the giant* fell asleep.

SONG: *(all)* "While the Giant Slept" (II)

SONG: *(all)* "That's the Story of Jack" (Reprise)

Student ______________________________ Date __________

Portfolio Evaluation Form

Directions: For each student, review the contents of the portfolio and assign a score of 1–4 for each criterion listed below. Determine a summary score for the entire portfolio, based on Criteria 1–12 (or more).

CONTENTS	Needs to Improve	Fair	Good	Excellent
1. **Completeness.** Meets all requirements.	1	2	3	4
2. **Variety.** Includes a variety of pieces.	1	2	3	4
3. **Organization.** Shows clear organizational plan.	1	2	3	4
4. **Volume.** Includes sufficient amount of work.	1	2	3	4
5. **Focus/Purpose.** Meets intended purposes.	1	2	3	4
ATTRIBUTES				
6. **Effort.** Demonstrates concerted effort.	1	2	3	4
7. **Quality.** Illustrates appropriate level of quality.	1	2	3	4
8. **Creativity.** Shows imagination and creative ideas.	1	2	3	4
9. **Risk-Taking.** Takes risks in creating/choosing works that go beyond minimum expectations.	1	2	3	4
10. **Growth.** Shows improvement.	1	2	3	4
11. **Reflection.** Shows signs of personal reflection.	1	2	3	4
12. **Self-Evaluation.** Shows awareness of strengths and weaknesses.	1	2	3	4
THINGS YOU'D LIKE TO ADD				
13. ______________________	1	2	3	4
14. ______________________	1	2	3	4
15. ______________________	1	2	3	4
SUMMARY SCORE				
Meets the requirements of program goals.	1	2	3	4

COMMENTS

Name ____________________

Student Assessment Cards

Directions: Help students complete one or more of these cards as an attachment for each item chosen for their portfolios.

Name of piece ____________________ Date __________

My description of this piece

Name of piece ____________________ Date __________

How I feel about this piece

Name ____________________ Date __________

RESOURCE MASTER TA•3 Tools for Assessment

Interest Inventory

Put a check beside as many answers as you like.

1. I like to. . .

_____ listen to music _____ move to music

_____ play music _____ make up music

_____ sing songs _____ perform for others

2. I'd like to know more about. . .

3. Here's an idea I'd like to try in music. . .

Name ______________________________ Date ______________

Self-Assessment Form

What I can do well	What I would like to do better
in listening	
in playing music	
in singing	
in moving to music	
in making up music	
in performing for others	

I'd like you to know. . .

Name ______________________ Grade __________

RESOURCE MASTER TA•5 Tools for Assessment

Music Log

Date	Title	What I Thought About It

Resource Master 1•6 page 8

TEST A:

1. kitten (soft)
2. singing voice
3. whispering voice

TEST B:

1. kitten (soft)
2. speaking voice
3. singing voice

Resource Master 2•5 page 17

TEST A:

1. patting beat
2. patting beat
3. short
4. long

TEST B:

1. patting beat
2. yawning/stretching
3. short
4. long

Resource Master 3•5 page 28

TEST A:

1. star (high)
2. starfish (low)
3. first pattern
4. walking
5. jogging

TEST B:

1. starfish (low)
2. star (high)
3. second pattern
4. jogging
5. walking

Resource Master 4•6 page 35

TEST A:

1. faster
2. faster
3. upward
4. downward
5. Pattern 2
6. Pattern 1

TEST B:

1. slower
2. slower
3. upward
4. downward
5. Pattern 1
6. Pattern 2

Resource Master 5•4 page 39

TEST A:

1. Beat 5
2. Beat 2
3. horse (galloping)
4. duck (walking)

Test B:

1. Beat 7
2. Beat 7
3. duck (walking)
4. horse (galloping)

Resource Master 6•4 page 44

TEST A:

1. one
2. two
3. different
4. same

TEST B:

1. two
2. one
3. same
4. different